UNITED WE DRINK

50 COCKTAIL RECIPES
Inspired by the
U.S. PRESIDENTS

WITH SARA MELLAS

HARPER
Celebrate

Cover illustrator: Jonathan Ball
Interior design: Emily Ghattas
Drink photography: Andrea Behrends
Food Stylist: Mayme Gretsch

Additional photography credits: all presidential portraits and remaining photography sourced from Library of Congress, except for the following: p. 132, Evan El-Amin/Shutterstock; p. 137, Serafima Antiopova/Shutterstock; p. 141, Marzufello/Shutterstock; and p. 145, alyaBigJoy/Shutterstock.

ISBN 978-1-4002-4920-6 (HC)
ISBN 978-1-4002-4916-9 (epub)

Printed in Vietnam
24 25 26 27 28 SEV 5 4 3 2 1

CONTENTS

I find friendship **TO BE LIKE WINE,** raw when new, ripened with age, the true old man's milk, **& RESTORATIVE CORDIAL.**

★ ★ ★ ★ ★ *Thomas Jefferson*

INTRODUCTION

From cocktails sipped in speakeasies, to beers downed at back-yard barbecues, to champagne toasts raised in celebration, few pastimes bring people together like sharing drinks. And for as long as regular Americans have been pouring, mixing, and enjoying alcohol, most of the presidents have as well. Although numerous presidents were known to be teetotal-ers, each president had drink preferences as unique as their political ideologies, and this book explores them all.

These recipes are a boozy testament to those who have carried the title of president of the United States. The cock-tails have been crafted in honor of the individual presidents, pulling lighthearted inspiration from their personalities, cam-paigns, and political careers, as well as anecdotes about their lives. With reimagined classics like martinis and gimlets, fruit-forward mixed drinks, frozen tiki bar–style favorites, and indulgent after-dinner sips, there is something for every taste and occasion. For those who avoid hard liquor, or who abstain from alcohol completely, you'll also find a handful of beer- and wine-based cocktails, and notes on how to make several of the recipes as nonalcoholic mocktails.

These drinks are meant to be effortlessly enjoyed, with many made from standard spirits and mixers you're likely to already have at home. Very few involve specialty alcohols and ingredients—no one likes to buy a large bottle of an obscure liqueur, only to use less than an ounce in a novelty cocktail— nor do they require fancy tools of any kind. If you have a basic cocktail shaker, jigger, stirrer, citrus juicer, and blender, you're already equipped to make every drink in this book. And because sooner is always better than later when it comes to cocktails, all of these can be mixed up in five minutes or less.

When it comes to serving, every recipe specifies the ideal glass in which to serve each cocktail, but, realistically, any drinking vessel will work just fine. Most also include suggestions for simple garnishes, which are always nice—but entirely optional—finishing touches.

Please feel free to use these recipes however they help you pursue the most happiness, but, as always, remember to drink responsibly. As you mix, shake, and drink your way through these pages, hopefully you'll gain some new pieces of historical trivia and have a few laughs along the way.

No matter what the current events or political landscape of America may be, this book invites you to enjoy, relax, and have a moment of taking it all a bit less seriously. With libations and justice for all, united we drink.

TRUE FRIENDSHIP

is a plant of

SLOW GROWTH.

★ ★ ★ ★ ★ *George Washington*

GEORGE WASHINGTON

FEDERALIST | 1789–1797

CHERRY NELSON

Remember that classic legend about our nation's first president, who purportedly became incapable of telling a lie after chopping down his father's cherry tree? Turns out it never happened! What is true, however, is that Washington, who was known to enjoy Caribbean rum, once attracted voters with dozens of gallons of rum during his campaign for the Virginia House of Burgesses. An accomplished horseman, he would have likely enjoyed this rum-based libation named for his favorite thoroughbred, Nelson.

★★★★★★★★★★★★★★★★★★ Makes 1 drink ★★★★★★★★★★★★★★★★★★

INGREDIENTS

2 ounces tart cherry juice

1 ounce dark rum

1 ounce cherry brandy

1 to 2 dashes Angostura bitters

2 cocktail cherries, for garnish

INSTRUCTIONS

1. Fill a mixing glass with ice.

2. Add the cherry juice, rum, cherry brandy, and bitters, and stir vigorously until chilled.

3. Strain into a rocks glass over fresh ice.

4. Skewer the cherries onto a toothpick and place in the glass. Enjoy.

JOHN ADAMS

FEDERALIST | 1797–1801

∾ MASSACHUSETTS MIMOSA ∾

John Adams loved hard cider. He loved it so much that he started every single morning with a cup of it, from the time he was sixteen years old. He wrote about "cyder" and its health benefits extensively in his letters, encouraging others to drink it liberally. The Massachusetts native also believed that local crops like cranberries and currants were particularly beneficial to the well-being of New Englanders. So, no matter where you're from or what time of day you prefer your boozy bubbles, go ahead and raise a toast to good health with this festive drink. John Adams would approve!

★ ★ ★ ★ ★ ★ ★ ★ ★ ★ ★ ★ ★ ★ ★ ★ Makes 1 drink ★ ★ ★ ★ ★ ★ ★ ★ ★ ★ ★ ★ ★ ★ ★ ★

INGREDIENTS

1 tablespoon frozen cranberries

1 ounce cranberry juice, chilled

3 ounces hard cider (apple)

INSTRUCTIONS

1. Place the frozen cranberries in a champagne flute and add the cranberry juice.

2. Top with the hard cider and enjoy.

John Adams

★ ★ ★ ★ ★

NO MAN

WHO EVER HELD

THE OFFICE OF

PRESIDENT WOULD

CONGRATULATE

A FRIEND

ON OBTAINING IT.

★ ★ ★ ★ ★

THOMAS JEFFERSON

DEMOCRATIC-REPUBLICAN | 1801–1809

MUSCADINE FLOAT

When he wasn't writing things like the Declaration of Independence, Thomas Jefferson wrote extensively about wine and food. A noted gourmand and oenophile, he loved wine. He loved it so much that he tried to grow his own grapes and make his own wine, all while nearly driving himself to bankruptcy by importing bottles from Europe. Jefferson was also the first American to write down a recipe for ice cream, and he helped popularize the dessert in the United States by serving it regularly at the President's House in Washington, DC—a celebratory societal contribution if there ever was one.

★ ★ ★ ★ ★ ★ ★ ★ ★ ★ ★ ★ ★ ★ ★   Makes 1 drink   ★ ★ ★ ★ ★ ★ ★ ★ ★ ★ ★ ★ ★ ★ ★

INGREDIENTS

5 ounces sweet red muscadine wine

1 large scoop vanilla ice cream

1½ to 2 ounces seltzer water

2 tablespoons fresh raspberries or cherries, pitted and halved (optional)

INSTRUCTIONS

1. Pour the wine into a wide-mouthed wineglass.

2. Add the generous scoop of ice cream and top with the seltzer water.

3. Add the raspberries or cherries to the glass, if desired.

4. Serve with a small dessert spoon and straw. Enjoy.

JAMES MADISON

DEMOCRATIC-REPUBLICAN | 1809–1817

∽ THE 1812 ∽

One part orange liqueur, four parts orange juice, four parts champagne, one orange slice, and two parts whiskey make for a sparkly cocktail with a historical punch line that's lost on everyone—but not on you! Or on James Madison, the champagne-loving president from Orange County, Virginia, who is perhaps best remembered for declaring the War of 1812. (Just be sure to follow the actual recipe below and not the playful puzzle above.)

★★★★★★★★★★★★★★★★★★★ Makes 1 drink ★★★★★★★★★★★★★★★★★★★

INGREDIENTS

2 ounces orange juice
1 ounce whiskey
½ ounce Cointreau or orange
    liqueur
2 ounces champagne or prosecco
1 orange slice, for garnish

INSTRUCTIONS

1. Fill a cocktail shaker with ice and add the orange juice, whiskey, and Cointreau. Shake vigorously until chilled.

2. Strain into a rocks glass over fresh ice and top with the champagne.

3. Garnish with the orange slice and enjoy.

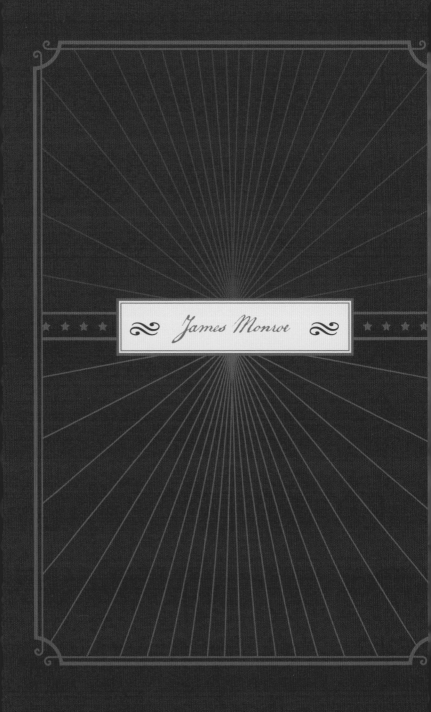

James Monroe

★ ★ ★ ★ ★

A LITTLE
FLATTERY
WILL
SUPPORT A
MAN
THROUGH
GREAT FATIGUE.

JAMES MONROE

DEMOCRATIC-REPUBLICAN | 1817–1825

∾ FRENCH FIVE ∾

Years before becoming president, James Monroe served as the minister to France. His Francophile ways stuck with him, and during his presidency he accidentally used funds Congress had reserved for buying furniture to import twelve hundred bottles of champagne and burgundy. It's safe to say the fifth president would have enjoyed this variation on the classic French 75 cocktail. Bon appétit!

★★★★★★★★★★★★★★★★★ **Makes 1 drink** ★★★★★★★★★★★★★★★★★

INGREDIENTS

½ ounce gin

½ ounce cognac

½ ounce fresh lemon juice

½ ounce simple syrup

2 ounces champagne or prosecco

1 lemon twist, for garnish

INSTRUCTIONS

1. Fill a cocktail shaker with ice and add the gin, cognac, lemon juice, and simple syrup. Shake vigorously until chilled.

2. Strain into a chilled champagne flute and top with the champagne.

3. Garnish with the lemon twist and enjoy.

JOHN QUINCY ADAMS

NATIONAL REPUBLICAN | 1825–1829

⊰ BLACKBERRY MOSCOW MULE ⊱

Said to have had the highest IQ of any president in U.S. history, John Quincy Adams could converse in multiple languages. While serving as minister to Russia prior to his presidency, JQA ditched the typical knee breeches and powdered wigs of the era in favor of long pants and a bald head, making him one of the first wigless Whigs.

Makes 1 drink

INGREDIENTS

4 to 5 fresh blackberries, plus 1 or 2 for garnish

½ ounce fresh lime juice

1½ ounces vodka

4 ounces ginger beer

1 sprig fresh mint, for garnish

INSTRUCTIONS

1. Place the blackberries and lime juice in a copper mug and muddle them together.

2. Add the vodka and fill the mug with crushed ice.

3. Pour in the ginger beer and stir gently to combine.

4. Garnish with the sprig of mint and a fresh blackberry or two, and *наслаждаться* (enjoy).

John Quincy Adams

★ ★ ★ ★ ★

MY TOAST WOULD BE, MAY OUR COUNTRY BE ALWAYS SUCCESSFUL, BUT WHETHER SUCCESSFUL OR OTHERWISE, ALWAYS RIGHT.

★ ★ ★ ★ ★

ANDREW JACKSON

DEMOCRAT | 1829–1837

OLD HICKORY'S STRAWBERRY SMASH

As the presidential candidate around whom the modern two-party system was formed, "Old Hickory" defined himself as a representative for the common man. Tennessee native Jackson was also fiercely defensive and, well, scrappy—engaging in occasional fatal duels, threatening to kill the bank, and making good on his promise to "smash" the Senate when they rejected his nomination for minister to England. The next time *you* feel the urge to smash the Senate, just grab some strawberries and make this drink instead.

★★★★★★★★★★★★★★★★★★★ Makes 1 drink ★★★★★★★★★★★★★★★★★★★

INGREDIENTS

4 fresh strawberries, rinsed

1/2 ounce fresh lemon juice

1/2 ounce simple syrup, or to taste

2 ounces Tennessee whiskey

2 to 3 ounces club soda

1 sprig fresh mint, for garnish

INSTRUCTIONS

1. Coarsely chop the strawberries and place them in a highball glass.

2. Add the lemon juice and simple syrup, and gently "smash" with a muddler until the berries are the consistency of compote. For a sweeter drink, add an additional 1/4 to 1/2 ounce of simple syrup.

3. Stir the whiskey into the muddled strawberries and fill a glass with crushed ice. Top with the club soda and stir gently.

4. Garnish with the sprig of fresh mint and enjoy.

MARTIN VAN BUREN

DEMOCRAT | 1837–1841

∾ BLUE VANHATTAN ∾

Martin Van Buren garnered many nicknames during his
time in office, one being "The Little Magician," for his
political cunning and social shrewdness, and another, "Blue
Whiskey Van," for how heavily he drank whiskey—a habit
he maintained all while establishing what is now known
as the Democratic Party. Naturally, the most appropriate
drink to pay homage to the first New York–born, whiskey-
loving president is a cerulean twist on a Manhattan.

★★★★★★★★★★★★★★★★★★★ Makes 1 drink ★★★★★★★★★★★★★★★★★★★★

INGREDIENTS

2 ounces rye whiskey

1/2 ounce sweet vermouth

1/2 ounce blue curaçao

2 dashes Angostura bitters

1 orange twist, for garnish

1 blue maraschino cherry, for
    garnish (optional)

INSTRUCTIONS

1. Pour the whiskey, vermouth,
    blue curaçao, and bitters into
    a mixing glass and fill the glass
    with ice. Stir vigorously until
    chilled.

2. Strain into a coupe glass.

3. Garnish with the orange twist
    and blue maraschino cherry, if
    desired, and enjoy.

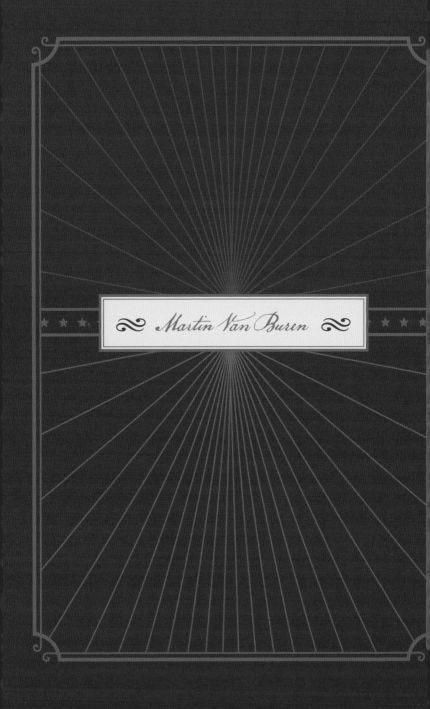

★ ★ ★ ★ ★

I WAS

**BORN FOR
A STORM,**

AND A CALM

DOES NOT

SUIT ME.

★ ★ ★ ★ ★

WILLIAM HENRY HARRISON

WHIG | 1841

~ OLD TIPP'S CIDER ~

Many argued that William Henry Harrison, at sixty-seven years of age, was too old to hold office, and they alleged he would do nothing but sit in his log cabin, drinking hard cider. The former military officer turned this mockery into the first modern election campaign slogan, winning the presidential seat on what was called the "Log Cabin and Hard Cider" campaign. Unfortunately, "Old Tipp" passed away after just thirty-one days as president, hardly giving him enough time to sit around and sip.

★★★★★★★★★★★★★★★★★★ Makes 1 drink ★★★★★★★★★★★★★★★★★★

INGREDIENTS

1 cinnamon stick
1½ ounces aged bourbon (the older, the better)
½ ounce fresh lemon juice
1 teaspoon maple syrup
4 ounces hard cider

INSTRUCTIONS

1. Place the cinnamon stick in a rocks glass and fill the glass with ice.
2. Fill a mixing glass with ice and pour in the bourbon, lemon juice, and maple syrup.
3. Stir thirty-one times.
4. Strain into the rocks glass, then top with the hard cider and enjoy.

JOHN TYLER

WHIG | 1841–1845

―――――――――――――

∽ SECOND-IN-COMMAND SPRITZ ∽

When Old Tipp passed away, Vice President John Tyler stepped
into the presidential role, marking the first time in American
history that a vice president took over the top job via the death
of the president. The administration of "His Accidency," as some
took to calling Tyler, was marked by quite a bit of controversy, and
he was eventually expelled from his own party. He was known
to enjoy a glass of champagne, and he no doubt enjoyed a glass
or two during his contentious tenure in the White House.

★★★★★★★★★★★★★★★★ Makes 1 drink ★★★★★★★★★★★★★★★★

INGREDIENTS

1 demerara sugar cube

½ ounce brandy

5½ ounces champagne or
    prosecco, chilled

1 orange twist, for garnish

INSTRUCTIONS

1. Place the sugar cube in a
    chilled champagne flute and
    add the brandy.

2. Top with the champagne.

3. Drop the orange twist in the
    glass and enjoy.

John Tyler

★ ★ ★ ★ ★

I SHOULD BE PLEASED
TO SEE ALL THE NATIONS
ON THE EARTH
PROSPEROUS AND
HAPPY AND RICH.

★ ★ ★ ★ ★

JAMES K. POLK

DEMOCRAT | 1845–1849

❦ THE DARK HORSE ❧

Former Tennessee governor James K. Polk is known for being the first "dark horse" presidential candidate, winning the election despite being widely unknown. During his time in office, he certainly put in his time—often twelve hours a day—and he took only twenty-seven days of vacation throughout his entire presidency. He's believed to have died of overwork in 1849. So the next time you find yourself working too hard, consider taking a break and stirring together this three-ingredient drink instead.

★★★★★★★★★★★★★★★★★★ Makes 1 drink ★★★★★★★★★★★★★★★★★★

INGREDIENTS

1½ ounces Tennessee whiskey

½ ounce Kahlúa

4½ ounces cola

1 lime wedge, for garnish

INSTRUCTIONS

1. Fill a highball glass with ice.

2. Add the whiskey, Kahlúa, and cola, and stir to combine.

3. Garnish with the lime wedge and enjoy.

ZACHARY TAYLOR

WHIG | 1849–1850

∿ ROUGH-AND-READY COFFEE ∿

Zachary Taylor was a major general in the United States Army, where he earned the nickname "Old Rough and Ready" on the battlefield. He was widely popular in both the Northern and Southern states, despite having no political affiliation, having never once voted, and, for all intents and purposes, having no ambition to be president. When first asked to run for office, Taylor allegedly responded, "Stop your nonsense and drink your whiskey!"

★★★★★★★★★★★★★★★★ Makes 1 drink ★★★★★★★★★★★★★★★★

INGREDIENTS

1 ounce Kahlúa

1 ounce whiskey

1 1/2 teaspoons brown sugar, plus more to taste

Dash of ground cinnamon

8 ounces hot strong-brewed coffee

Whipped cream, for topping (optional)

INSTRUCTIONS

1. Place the Kahlúa, whiskey, brown sugar, and cinnamon in a large mug and stir to combine.

2. Pour in the hot coffee.

3. Top with a generous amount of whipped cream, if desired, and enjoy.

James Polk

★ ★ ★ ★ ★

WE REJOICE IN THE
GENERAL
HAPPINESS,
PROSPERITY, AND
ADVANCEMENT
OF OUR COUNTRY,
WHICH HAVE BEEN
THE OFFSPRING OF
FREEDOM.

★ ★ ★ ★ ★

MILLARD FILLMORE

WHIG | 1850–1853

～ AMERICA-KNOW NOTHING ～

With Millard Fillmore's presidency came the disintegration of the Whig Party, and after leaving office he was uninterested in joining the Republican Party. Instead, he quietly became a member of the short-lived "Know Nothing" Party, earning their nomination for the 1856 election. With bitter Campari, sweet vermouth, and a touch of citrus, this refreshing cocktail goes down as swiftly as an obscure political party in the mid-1800s.

★★★★★★★★★★★★★★★★★★★ Makes 1 drink ★★★★★★★★★★★★★★★★★★★

INGREDIENTS

1½ ounces Campari

1½ ounces sweet vermouth

2 ounces orange or unflavored seltzer water

1-inch strip of orange peel, for garnish

INSTRUCTIONS

1. Fill a highball glass with ice and add the Campari and vermouth.

2. Top with the seltzer water and stir to combine.

3. Twist the orange peel over the glass and drop it in. Enjoy.

FRANKLIN PIERCE

DEMOCRAT | 1853–1857

∿ PUMPKIN ALEXANDER ∿

Outside of his single controversial presidential term,
Pierce was born, died, and spent most of his life in New
Hampshire, where his father served as governor for two
terms. This autumnal variation on a Brandy Alexander
features a bit of pumpkin, the official fruit of the state.

★ ★ ★ ★ ★ ★ ★ ★ ★ ★ ★ ★ ★ ★ ★   Makes 1 drink   ★ ★ ★ ★ ★ ★ ★ ★ ★ ★ ★ ★ ★ ★ ★

INGREDIENTS

1 teaspoon pumpkin puree

Dash of pumpkin pie spice, plus
more for sprinkling

1 ounce light or heavy cream

1 ounce crème de cacao

¾ ounce cognac

INSTRUCTIONS

1. Place the pumpkin puree,
    pumpkin pie spice, cream,
    crème de cacao, and cognac
    in a cocktail shaker and shake
    vigorously to combine.

2. Fill the shaker with ice and
    continue shaking until chilled.

3. Strain into a coupe glass.

4. Sprinkle with a pinch of
    pumpkin pie spice and enjoy.

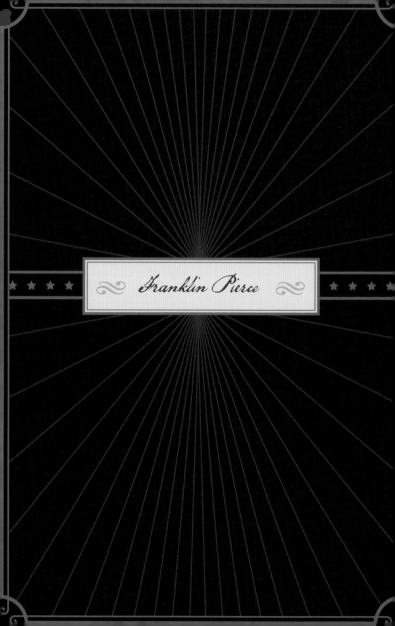

Franklin Pierce

★ ★ ★ ★ ★

THERE'S NOTHING LEFT...BUT TO GET DRUNK.

★ ★ ★ ★ ★

JAMES BUCHANAN

DEMOCRAT | 1857–1861

∽ PENNSYLVANIA SOUR ∽

The one and only president hailing from Pennsylvania, James Buchanan took office at one of the sourest times in United States history. Being the president to precede the outbreak of the Civil War, his term has never won history's popular vote. Today, you can visit his boyhood home in Mercersburg, Pennsylvania, which has now been adapted into the James Buchanan Hotel.

★★★★★★★★★★★★★★★★★ Makes 1 drink ★★★★★★★★★★★★★★★★★

INGREDIENTS

2 ounces single malt scotch

3/4 ounce fresh lemon juice

1/2 ounce simple syrup

1 tablespoon egg white (optional)

1/2 ounce sweet red wine

1-inch strip of lemon peel, for garnish

INSTRUCTIONS

1. Place the scotch, lemon juice, simple syrup, and egg white (if desired) in a cocktail shaker and shake vigorously until frothy.

2. Fill the shaker with ice and continue shaking until chilled.

3. Strain into a rocks glass over fresh ice.

4. Drizzle the red wine into the glass, letting it float on top.

5. Twist the lemon peel over the glass, then drop it in. Enjoy.

ABRAHAM LINCOLN

REPUBLICAN | 1861–1865

APPLE ROSEMARY GIN AND TONIC

One of the most significant presidents in United States history, Honest Abe was a self-made man who presided over the nation through the Civil War, ultimately leading the country toward unification. A sober individual in every sense of the word, Lincoln was known for such curiosities as eating whole apples—core, seeds, and stem included—and being extremely tall for the era. Standing at six feet four inches *without* his signature top hat, he was one tall drink of tonic water.

★★★★★★★★★★★★★★★★★★★ Makes 1 drink ★★★★★★★★★★★★★★★★★★★

INGREDIENTS

1½ ounces gin

1 ounce apple juice

5 to 7 thin apple slices, plus 1 for garnish

1 sprig rosemary, cut into 3 segments

4 ounces tonic water

To make a Lincoln-approved mocktail, omit the gin and increase the apple juice to 2½ ounces.

INSTRUCTIONS

1. Pour the gin and apple juice into a tall glass and stir to combine.

2. Fill the glass about one-quarter of the way with ice.

3. Add an apple slice and a rosemary segment. Repeat twice more until the glass is almost full, then pour in the tonic water. Stir gently.

4. Garnish with the remaining apple slice and enjoy through a straw.

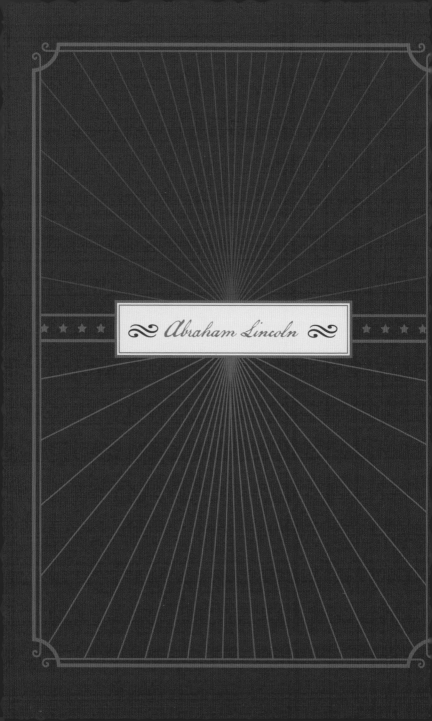

≈ *Abraham Lincoln* ≈

★ ★ ★ ★ ★

THE
BETTER
PART OF
ONE'S LIFE
CONSISTS
OF HIS
FRIENDSHIPS.

★ ★ ★ ★ ★

ANDREW JOHNSON

DEMOCRAT | 1865–1869

∾ COLD CRUSHER ∾

During his 1865 vice presidential inauguration under the Lincoln administration, Andrew Johnson reportedly showed up to the ceremony so drunk that he was slurring his words. As the story goes, he assured his fellow politicians that he had come down with a bad cold and treated it with whiskey. This spicy hot drink may or may not be the perfect cure for the next time you get the sniffles.

★★★★★★★★★★★★★★★★★ Makes 1 drink ★★★★★★★★★★★★★★★★★★★

INGREDIENTS

¼-inch piece fresh gingerroot, peeled and grated (about ½ teaspoon)

1 tablespoon honey

Dash of cayenne pepper (optional)

2 ounces whiskey

6 ounces very hot water

Juice from 1 large lemon wedge

1 lemon slice, for garnish

INSTRUCTIONS

1. Clear your schedule of any important meetings or historical events.

2. Place the grated ginger, honey, and cayenne in a large mug.

3. Pour in the whiskey and hot water.

4. Add the squeeze of lemon juice and stir well to combine.

5. Garnish with the lemon slice and enjoy.

ULYSSES S. GRANT

REPUBLICAN | 1869–1877

∽ UNION GIMLET ∽

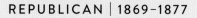

Most famously known as the commanding general of the
Union Army who claimed victory in the Civil War, Grant
led the country through Reconstruction and helped enact the
Fifteenth Amendment during his two presidential terms. As
president, he upheld his strategic and straightforward nature,
for better or worse, and once accused his outspoken naysayers
of being "narrow-headed men [with eyes so close together]
they can look out of the same gimlet hole without winking."

★ ★ ★ ★ ★ ★ ★ ★ ★ ★ ★ ★ ★ ★ ★ ★ ★ Makes 1 drink ★ ★ ★ ★ ★ ★ ★ ★ ★ ★ ★ ★ ★ ★ ★ ★ ★

INGREDIENTS

2 ounces gin
3/4 ounce simple syrup
1/2 ounce fresh lemon juice
1/2 ounce fresh lime juice

INSTRUCTIONS

1. Fill a cocktail shaker with ice
   and add the gin, simple syrup,
   lemon juice, and lime juice.
   Shake vigorously to combine.

2. Strain into a chilled coupe glass
   and enjoy.

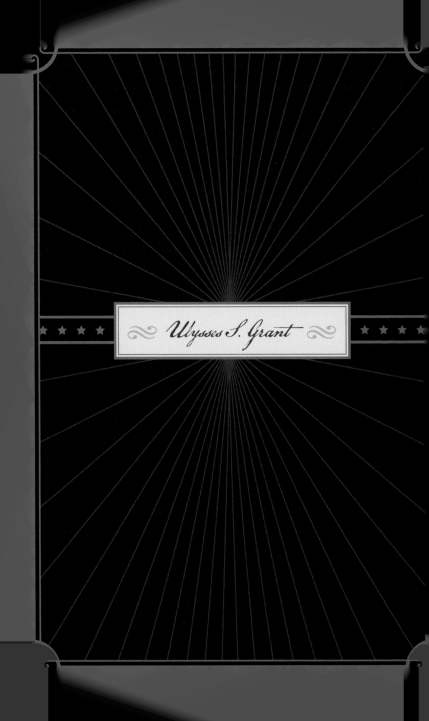

Ulysses S. Grant

* * ★ * *

I KNOW ONLY
TWO TUNES:
ONE OF THEM IS
"YANKEE
DOODLE,"
AND THE
OTHER ISN'T.

* * ★ * *

· ★ ★ ★ **NO. 19** ★ ★ ★ ·

RUTHERFORD B. HAYES

REPUBLICAN | 1877–1881

∽ RUTHERFORD RUM PUNCH ∽

As First Lady Lucy Webb Hayes was a noted teetotaler, the White House was alcohol-free for the duration of Rutherford's presidential term. However, rumor has it that certain staff members would infuse orange slices with rum and add them to Roman Punch for guests. Hayes contested this claim by insisting the punch had only been flavored with extracts to emulate Jamaican rum.

★ ★ ★ ★ ★ ★ ★ ★ ★ ★ ★ ★ ★ ★ ★ ★ Makes 4 drinks ★ ★ ★ ★ ★ ★ ★ ★ ★ ★ ★ ★ ★ ★ ★ ★ ★

INGREDIENTS

1 large orange

8 ounces light rum

8 ounces orange juice

8 ounces pineapple juice

2 ounces grenadine

2 ounces fresh lemon juice

4 pineapple wedges, for garnish

4 maraschino or cocktail
  cherries, for garnish

If you're like Lucy and prefer a nonalcoholic drink, replace the rum in this recipe with an equal amount of club soda.

INSTRUCTIONS

1. Peel the orange and cut it into ¼-inch-thick slices. Cut each slice into quarters. Set aside.

2. Pour the rum, orange juice, pineapple juice, grenadine, and lemon juice into a small pitcher and stir vigorously to combine. Add the orange segments.

3. Fill four glasses with ice and divide the punch evenly among them.

4. Garnish with the pineapple wedges and cherries. Enjoy.

JAMES GARFIELD

REPUBLICAN | 1881

EL DIABLO

Though his term was tragically cut short, Garfield sought to eradicate the political corruption that had become widespread in the country's recent history, stating, "It is a brave man . . . who dares to look the devil in the face and tell him he is a devil."

★★★★★★★★★★★★★★★★★★★★ Makes 1 drink ★★★★★★★★★★★★★★★★★★★★

INGREDIENTS

1 1/2 ounces reposado tequila
1/2 ounce crème de cassis (or Chambord)
1/2 ounce fresh lime juice
2 1/2 to 3 ounces ginger beer
1 lime wedge, for garnish

INSTRUCTIONS

1. Fill a cocktail shaker with ice and add the tequila, crème de cassis, and lime juice. Shake vigorously until chilled.

2. Strain into a highball glass over fresh ice.

3. Add the ginger beer and stir to combine.

4. Garnish with the lime wedge and enjoy.

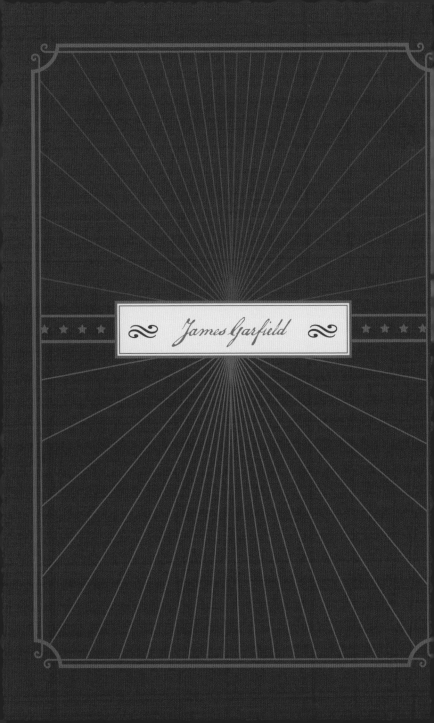

James Garfield

★ ★ ★ ★ ★

THINGS DON'T
TURN UP IN
THIS WORLD
UNTIL SOMEBODY
TURNS THEM UP.

★ ★ ★ ★ ★

CHESTER A. ARTHUR

REPUBLICAN | 1881–1885

∽ IRISH HOT CHOCOLATE ∽

Chester A. Arthur, the son of an Irish preacher, was a connoisseur of the finer things in life. He would often have chocolate cake served at White House dinners—an indulgence almost as good as this boozy, smooth homemade hot chocolate.

★ ★ ★ ★ ★ ★ ★ ★ ★ ★ ★ ★ ★ Makes 2 drinks ★ ★ ★ ★ ★ ★ ★ ★ ★ ★ ★ ★ ★

INGREDIENTS

2 ounces Irish cream liqueur, divided

2 ounces dark chocolate (70 to 75 percent), roughly chopped

1 tablespoon unsweetened cocoa powder

1 to 2 teaspoons granulated sugar

12 ounces whole milk

Dash of salt

Whipped cream, for serving (optional)

Almond, oat, or coconut milk may be used instead of whole milk.

INSTRUCTIONS

1. Fill two mugs with 1 ounce each of Irish cream liqueur and set aside.

2. Place the chocolate, cocoa powder, sugar, milk, and salt in a small saucepan and set it over medium-high heat.

3. Once the milk begins to steam, whisk steadily until the chocolate is fully melted and the cocoa and sugar are dissolved. Continue whisking until the milk gently bubbles around the edges, then remove the saucepan from heat.

4. Pour the hot chocolate into the mugs.

5. Top with a generous amount of whipped cream, if desired, and enjoy.

GROVER CLEVELAND

DEMOCRAT | 1885–1889, 1893–1897

∽ DOUBLE CITRUS SHANDY ∽

Grover Cleveland served two separate terms as president. Prior to his presidencies, when he was the mayor of Buffalo and governor of New York, Cleveland was a fixture in local bars, where he would drink up to a *gallon* of beer a day. Perhaps he would have benefitted from cutting his pints with a bit of juice, like in this refreshing and puckery two-citrus shandy.

★★★★★★★★★★★★★★★★★★ Makes 1 drink ★★★★★★★★★★★★★★★★★★

INGREDIENTS

3 ounces grapefruit juice

3 ounces sparkling lemon soda

6 ounces wheat beer or pilsner

1 lemon slice, for garnish

1 grapefruit slice, for garnish

INSTRUCTIONS

1. Pour the grapefruit juice into a pilsner glass, followed by the lemon soda and beer.

2. Garnish with the lemon slice and grapefruit slice and enjoy.

Benjamin Harrison

★ ★ ★ ★ ★

GREAT LIVES

NEVER GO OUT;

THEY GO ON.

★ ★ ★ ★ ★

BENJAMIN HARRISON

REPUBLICAN | 1889–1893

~ BUCKEYE ~

As the grandson of ninth president William Henry Harrison and the great-grandson of Founding Father Benjamin Harrison V, Benjamin Harrison was simply carrying on the family business when he assumed the role of leader of the nation. While in office, he added six northwestern states to the country, but it was in Ohio—the Buckeye State—that he began his life and career. Like the confection, this decadent dessert cocktail features the perfect pairing of peanut butter and chocolate.

Makes 1 drink

INGREDIENTS

2 ounces half-and-half

1 ounce peanut butter whiskey

1 ounce dark crème de cacao

1¹/2 teaspoons chocolate syrup, plus more for drizzling

INSTRUCTIONS

1. Fill a cocktail shaker with ice and add the half-and-half, whiskey, crème de cacao, and chocolate syrup. Shake vigorously until combined and chilled.

2. Drizzle chocolate syrup around the inside edges of a rocks glass and fill the glass with ice.

3. Strain the chilled drink into the glass and enjoy.

WILLIAM MCKINLEY

REPUBLICAN | 1897–1901

GRASSHOPPER

William McKinley was elected president in 1896 on a successful front-porch campaign, which sparked the creation of a new rye whiskey–based cocktail—the McKinley's Delight. Once in office, he devoted considerable time to bickering with other men over the pros and cons of silver versus gold, and a House Speaker once commented that McKinley kept his ear so close to the ground that it was "full of grasshoppers." This money-green, cool dessert cocktail may just become your new gold standard of after-dinner drinks.

★★★★★★★★★★★★★★★★ Makes 1 drink ★★★★★★★★★★★★★★★★

INGREDIENTS

2 ounces light or heavy cream

3/4 ounce crème de menthe

1 ounce white crème de cacao

1 square mint chocolate, for garnish (optional)

INSTRUCTIONS

1. Pour the cream, crème de menthe, and crème de cacao into a cocktail shaker and shake vigorously until frothy.

2. Fill the shaker halfway with ice and shake again until chilled.

3. Strain into a martini glass.

4. Use a hand grater to shave the square of chocolate over the top, for garnish, if desired. Enjoy and prosper.

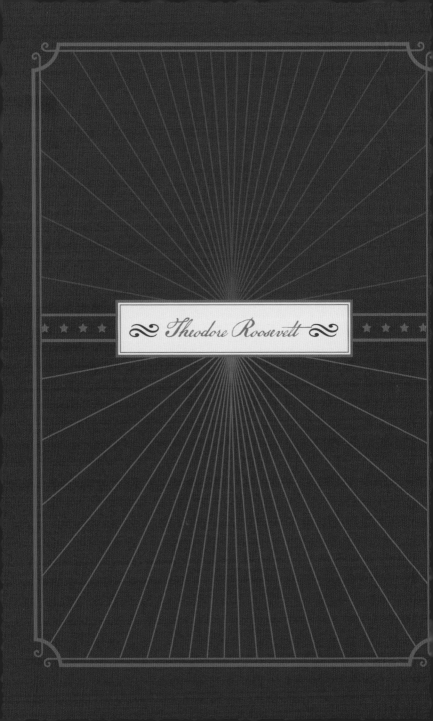

* ★ ★ ★ ★ *

SPEAK SOFTLY

AND CARRY A

BIG STICK;

YOU WILL
GO FAR.

* ★ ★ ★ *

THEODORE ROOSEVELT

REPUBLICAN | 1901–1909

∽ HOT TEDDY ∽

Theodore Roosevelt was a practitioner of what he called "the strenuous life," believing that character is built by working hard and facing challenges head-on. For example, from early childhood, he would test himself by jumping into ice-cold rivers in midwinter or challenging compatriots to boxing matches. Teddy was a fan of mint juleps, but with all that strenuousness, he probably could have used a relaxing hot drink every once in a while.

Makes 1 drink

INGREDIENTS

3 leaves fresh mint

6 ounces very hot water

2 ounces bourbon

2 to 3 teaspoons honey, to taste

2 to 3 teaspoons fresh lemon
juice, to taste

1 sprig fresh mint, for garnish

INSTRUCTIONS

1. Place the mint leaves in a large mug and pour in the hot water. Stir, muddling the mint against the bottom of the mug.

2. Add the bourbon and stir in the honey and lemon juice, to taste.

3. Garnish with the sprig of fresh mint, drink up, and enjoy.

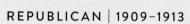

WILLIAM HOWARD TAFT

REPUBLICAN | 1909–1913

∽ MANILA BRONX ∾

In his life, William Howard Taft served both as president and later as chief justice of the United States. One job he loved, and the other he did not, writing in his later years, "I don't remember that I ever was president." In 1911 Taft and his friends caused a small scandal at a restaurant in St. Louis when they ordered a round of Bronx cocktails during breakfast—an unseemly hour to be drinking publicly, by the early twentieth century's brunchless standards. This mango twist on the Bronx is in honor of the Philippines, where Taft began his career in government.

★★★★★★★★★★★★★★★★★★★★ Makes 1 drink ★★★★★★★★★★★★★★★★★★★★

INGREDIENTS

2 ounces gin
2 ounces mango juice or orange-
    mango juice
¼ ounce dry vermouth
¼ ounce sweet vermouth
Dash of orange bitters (optional)
1 fresh mango slice, for garnish

INSTRUCTIONS

1. Fill a cocktail shaker with ice and add the gin, mango juice, dry vermouth, sweet vermouth, and bitters. Shake vigorously until chilled.

2. Strain into a chilled martini glass.

3. Garnish with the slice of fresh mango and enjoy.

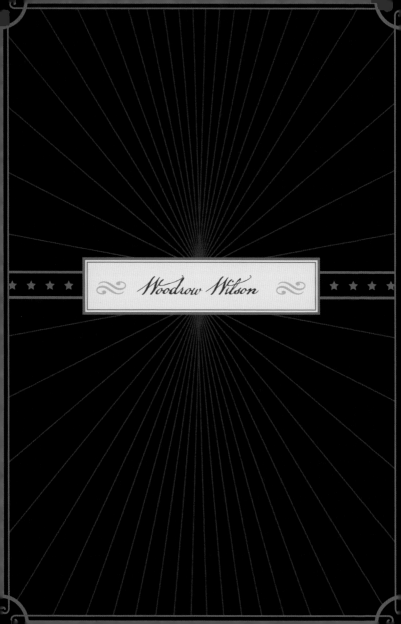

Woodrow Wilson

★ ★ ★ ★ ★

I NOT ONLY USE ALL THE BRAINS I HAVE, BUT ALL I CAN BORROW.

★ ★ ★ ★ ★

WOODROW WILSON

DEMOCRAT | 1913–1921

∽ WHISKEY, THAT'S ALL ∽

Woodrow Wilson won the presidential election to the tune
of his campaign song, "Wilson, That's All." The song was
inspired by Wilson Whiskey, a popular brand in the early
twentieth century, making it slightly ironic that he was the
president in office during the enactment of Prohibition. To
be fair, Wilson enjoyed a good scotch and had vetoed the act
that would illegalize booze, but he was overridden by sixty-
five buzzkill senators. This drink, which combines scotch and
scotch-based liqueur, is technically known as a Rusty Nail, but
one could say that's just bartenderspeak for "all whiskey."

★★★★★★★★★★★★★★★★★★ Makes 1 drink ★★★★★★★★★★★★★★★★★★

INGREDIENTS

1½ ounces scotch

1 ounce Drambuie

Whiskey ice cube (optional,
    allow time for freezing)

1-inch strip of lemon peel, for
    garnish

INSTRUCTIONS

1. Place the scotch and Drambuie in
    a rocks glass and add the ice cube.

2. Stir one time for each of the
    fourteen points that Wilson
    proposed for peace following the
    ravages of World War I.

3. Twist the lemon peel over the
    drink, then drop it in. That's all—
    enjoy.

WARREN G. HARDING

REPUBLICAN | 1921–1923

SPIKED RASPBERRY ICED TEA

Warren G. Harding accomplished many things during his presidency. He established the country's first formal budgeting process, signed off on the first social welfare program, orchestrated the Teapot Dome scandal—one of the largest political scandals in United States history—and more. Enough of all that; mix up one of these cocktails, and focus on the positive!

★★★★★★★★★★★★★★★ Makes 1 drink ★★★★★★★★★★★★★★★

INGREDIENTS

1½ ounces raspberry vodka

½ ounce Chambord or raspberry liqueur

6 ounces sweetened brewed iced tea

1 lemon slice, for garnish

INSTRUCTIONS

1. Fill a tall glass with ice and add the vodka and Chambord.

2. Top with the iced tea and stir to combine.

3. Garnish with the slice of lemon. Enjoy with loyal friends.

To make a batch of 6 to 8 servings, stir together ¾ cup vodka, ½ cup Chambord, and 6 cups iced tea in a large pitcher. Divide among glasses filled with ice.

NO PERSON WAS EVER

HONORED

FOR WHAT HE

RECEIVED. HONOR HAS

BEEN THE REWARD FOR

WHAT HE GAVE.

CALVIN COOLIDGE

REPUBLICAN | 1923–1929

❧ SILENT THIRTY ❧

Calvin Coolidge was known for his economical and straightforward approach to both politics and speaking. He famously earned the nickname "Silent Cal" for how discriminating he was with words. However, he was known for his dry wit, once saying, "I think the American public wants a solemn ass as a President—and I think I'll go along with them." This simple cocktail is a variation on the Silent Third, made fit for the thirtieth president.

★ Makes 1 drink ★

INGREDIENTS

1¼ ounces vodka
1 ounce Cointreau or Grand Marnier
¾ ounce fresh lemon juice

INSTRUCTIONS

1. Fill a cocktail shaker with ice and add the vodka, Cointreau, and lemon juice. Shake vigorously until chilled.

2. Strain into a chilled coupe or martini glass and enjoy.

HERBERT HOOVER

REPUBLICAN | 1929–1933

～ WICKERSHAM MARTINI ～

Many remember Herbert Hoover as the president who was in office during the unfortunate years of the Great Depression, but he was also a passionate humanitarian who effectively helped prevent and alleviate hunger in the United States and Europe during World War I. While Hoover publicly supported Prohibition, he privately enjoyed wine and dry martinis. He was even friends with Hugh Gibson, namesake of the onion-garnished Gibson martini.

★★★★★★★★★★★★★★★★★★★ Makes 1 drink ★★★★★★★★★★★★★★★★★★★

INGREDIENTS

2¹/₂ ounces gin or vodka
¹/₂ ounce dry vermouth
2 cocktail onions, for garnish
1 Spanish green olive, for garnish

INSTRUCTIONS

1. Fill a mixing glass with ice and add the gin and dry vermouth. Stir until chilled.
2. Strain into a chilled martini glass.
3. Skewer the onions and olive onto a toothpick, with the olive in the middle, and place the toothpick in the drink. Enjoy.

Franklin Delano Roosevelt

IF YOU TREAT PEOPLE RIGHT, THEY WILL TREAT YOU RIGHT ... NINETY PERCENT OF THE TIME.

FRANKLIN DELANO ROOSEVELT

DEMOCRAT | 1933–1945

⤳ TWELVE-YEAR RUM SWIZZLE ⤳

Twelve years is a long time to stay at any one job, especially when that job is president of the United States, and the primary duties are to save the country from the largest economic crisis in its history and navigate worldwide war. It's a wonder FDR had time to host intimate cocktail hours where he was known to mix up adventurous concoctions for his closest friends. One of his favorites was his own personal take on a Bermuda Rum Swizzle.

Makes 1 drink

INGREDIENTS

2 ounces twelve-year aged rum

2 ounces orange juice

2 ounces pineapple juice

¼ ounce simple syrup

¼ ounce fresh lime juice

2 dashes Angostura bitters

Dash of allspice

1 orange slice, for garnish

1 pineapple wedge, for garnish

1 cocktail cherry, for garnish

INSTRUCTIONS

1. Fill a cocktail shaker with ice and add the rum, orange juice, pineapple juice, simple syrup, lime juice, bitters, and allspice. Shake vigorously until chilled.

2. Strain into a highball or hurricane glass over crushed ice.

3. Garnish with an orange slice, pineapple wedge, and cocktail cherry, and sip through a straw. Enjoy.

HARRY TRUMAN

DEMOCRAT | 1945–1953

❧ FAIR OLD-FASHIONED ❧

Few presidents have served amid such unprecedented global circumstances, and the efforts and decisions Harry Truman made during his time in the White House carried a profound, long-standing impact. With a daily agenda like the one Truman had, it's somewhat understandable that he liked to start his mornings with a shot of bourbon. He was also partial to the classic Old-Fashioned and was known to speak up if he felt it wasn't strong enough!

★★★★★★★★★★★★★★★★★★★ Makes 1 drink ★★★★★★★★★★★★★★★★★★★

INGREDIENTS

1 teaspoon fine granulated sugar
1 teaspoon water
2 to 3 dashes Angostura bitters
Whiskey ice cube (optional, allow time for freezing)
2½ ounces high-proof bourbon
1-inch strip of orange peel, for garnish
1 cocktail cherry, for garnish

INSTRUCTIONS

1. Place the sugar, water, and bitters in a rocks glass and give it hell with a cocktail stirrer until the sugar is dissolved.

2. Place the ice cube in the glass. Pour in the bourbon and stir once more.

3. Twist the orange peel over the drink and drop it in.

4. Garnish with the cherry and enjoy.

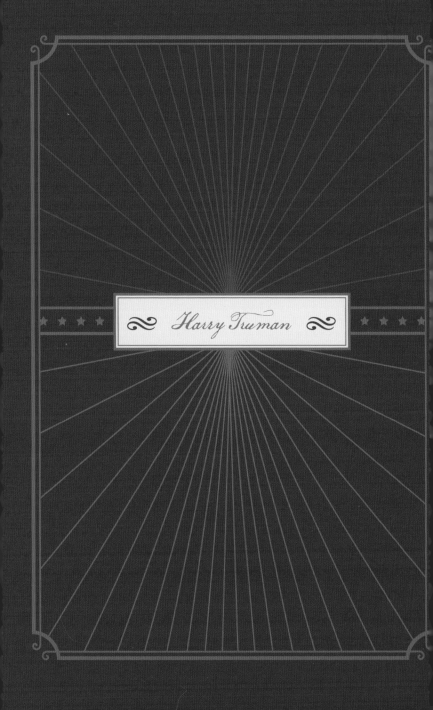

Harry Truman

IT IS AMAZING
WHAT YOU CAN
ACCOMPLISH
IF YOU DO NOT
CARE WHO GETS
THE CREDIT.

DWIGHT D. EISENHOWER

REPUBLICAN | 1953–1961

∽ MEZCAL MARGARITA ∾

Dwight D. Eisenhower came into his presidency after a long career of military successes. However, his life almost went in a very different direction, as he originally intended to move to Argentina, after graduating military school, to become a gaucho. However, Ike stayed and went on to change the course of history with his military expertise, all while chain-smoking three to four packs of cigarettes a day. No doubt he'd love this simple, smoky marg.

★ ★ ★ ★ ★ ★ ★ ★ ★ ★ ★ ★ ★ ★ ★ ★ Makes 1 drink ★ ★ ★ ★ ★ ★ ★ ★ ★ ★ ★ ★ ★ ★ ★ ★

INGREDIENTS

Kosher salt, for the glass rim

1 lime slice, for garnish

3 ounces mezcal

1½ ounces fresh lime juice

1½ ounces Cointreau

½ to ¾ ounce agave nectar (optional)

1 lime slice, for garnish

If this Mezcal Margarita is too smoky for your taste, feel free to use your favorite tequila instead.

INSTRUCTIONS

1. Shake a bit of kosher salt onto a plate. Run the lime wedge around the rim of a rocks or margarita glass, then dip the rim into the salt, rotating the glass until its perimeter is evenly coated. Fill the glass with ice and set aside.

2. Fill a cocktail shaker with ice and add the mezcal, lime juice, Cointreau, and agave nectar, if desired. Shake vigorously to combine.

3. Strain into the rimmed glass.

4. Garnish with a lime slice and enjoy.

JOHN F. KENNEDY

DEMOCRAT | 1961–1963

❧ FROZEN STRAWBERRY JACKUIRI ❧

JFK perhaps drew more public intrigue than any president before him, becoming a celebrity in a way that was previously reserved for actors and musicians. Americans took as much interest in his personal life as his political one, so when word got out that his staff had set up the first-ever bar in the State Dining Room, countless strongly worded letters flooded into the White House's mailbox. These didn't stop Jack from the occasional enjoyment of his favorite cocktail—a daiquiri.

★ ★ ★ ★ ★ ★ ★ ★ ★ ★ ★ ★ ★ ★ ★ ★ ★ Makes 2 drinks ★ ★ ★ ★ ★ ★ ★ ★ ★ ★ ★ ★ ★ ★ ★ ★ ★

INGREDIENTS

8 ounces (1¼ cups) frozen strawberries

4 ounces white rum

2 ounces fresh lime juice

2 ounces simple syrup

1 fresh strawberry, halved, for garnish

2 lime slices, for garnish

INSTRUCTIONS

1. Place the frozen strawberries, rum, lime juice, and simple syrup in a blender and blend until smooth. For an icier drink, add ½ to ¾ cup ice cubes. Divide between two chilled punch glasses.

2. Garnish each with the strawberry half and a lime slice and enjoy through straws.

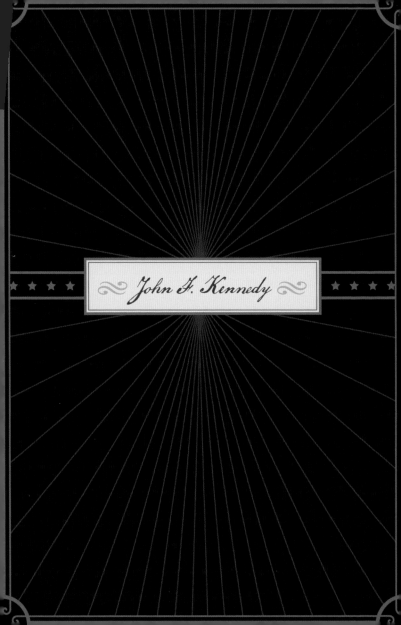

John F. Kennedy

★ ★ ★ ★ ★

A
RISING TIDE
LIFTS ALL
BOATS.

★ ★ ★ ★ ★

LYNDON B. JOHNSON

DEMOCRAT | 1963–1969

～ THE GS ～

Like a true Southerner, Lyndon B. Johnson monogrammed many of his belongings and also gave names to his children and dog that shared his initials. LBJ is often remembered for the hugely impactful Great Society programs he pushed through Congress, and less often remembered for his pastime of drinking scotch out of a plastic cup while driving at high speeds around his Texas ranch. Feel free to mix this drink in a plastic cup of your own. Just be sure to enjoy more responsibly than the former president!

Makes 1 drink

INGREDIENTS

2 ounces scotch

4 ounces ginger beer

1 lime slice, for garnish

INSTRUCTIONS

1. Fill a highball glass or plastic cup with ice and add the scotch. Pour in the ginger beer and stir to combine.

2. Garnish with the lime slice and enjoy seated or standing, far from motorized vehicles.

NO. 37 ★ ★ ★

RICHARD NIXON

REPUBLICAN | 1969–1974

THE RICKEY NIX

During Richard Nixon's time as president, NASA successfully landed Apollo 11 on the moon. Despite the nation's triumphs in these years, what goes up must come down. Nixon remains the only president to have ever resigned from office. Fortunately, this simple cocktail is far from tricky to make, so let it bubble up, then drink it down.

★★★★★★★★★★★★★★★★ Makes 1 drink ★★★★★★★★★★★★★★★★

INGREDIENTS

1½ ounces gin or vodka
½ ounce fresh lime juice
3 ounces seltzer water
1 lime wedge, for garnish

INSTRUCTIONS

1. Pour the gin and lime juice into a highball glass and fill the glass with ice. Add the seltzer water and stir to combine.

2. Garnish with the lime wedge and enjoy.

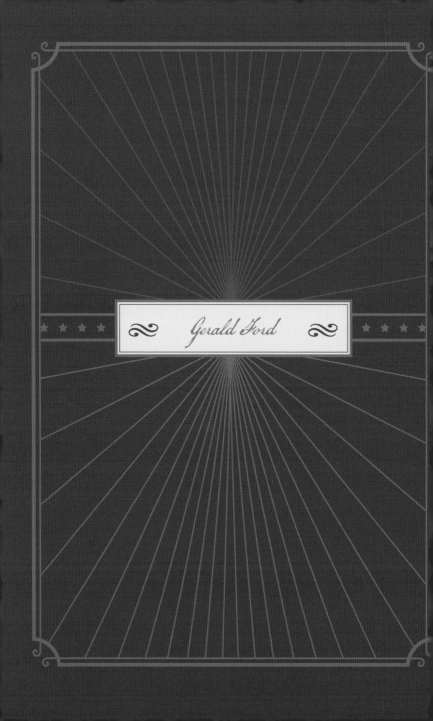

* * ★ * *

TELL THE TRUTH,

WORK HARD,

AND COME

TO DINNER

ON TIME.

* * ★ * *

GERALD FORD

REPUBLICAN | 1974–1977

∾ THE FIX ∾

When Ford stepped into office, he had a lot of work ahead of him: improving the economy, curbing inflation, repairing foreign relationships, boosting national morale, and more. This drink won't make your problems go away, but it *is* much easier to fix than all the ails of the nation.

★★★★★★★★★★★★★★★★★ Makes 1 drink ★★★★★★★★★★★★★★★★★

INGREDIENTS

2 ounces gin, whiskey, or brandy

1 ounce fresh lemon juice

1 ounce pineapple juice

1/2 ounce simple syrup

1 lemon slice, for garnish

INSTRUCTIONS

1. Fill a cocktail shaker with ice and add your alcohol of choice from the recommended ingredients, the lemon juice, the pineapple juice, and the simple syrup. Shake vigorously until chilled.

2. Strain into a rocks glass over crushed ice.

3. Garnish with the lemon slice and enjoy.

★ ★ ★ **NO. 39** ★ ★ ★

JIMMY CARTER

DEMOCRAT | 1977–1981

❧ PEACEFUL PEACH SPRITZER ❧

Few presidents have fought for international human rights in the way Jimmy Carter has, and his efforts won him the Nobel Peace Prize in 2002. Perhaps his commitment to world peace is what has helped him become the longest-living president in history. Or perhaps it's the fact that he rarely drinks alcohol. When the Georgia native *does* reach for a drink, he reportedly chooses white wine, which tastes especially refreshing when poured over frozen peach slices and topped off with bubbles.

★★★★★★★★★★★★★★★★★★ Makes 1 drink ★★★★★★★★★★★★★★★★★★

INGREDIENTS

4 to 5 frozen peach slices

6 ounces sweet white wine

2 ounces peach seltzer water

INSTRUCTIONS

1. Place the peach slices in a chilled wineglass.

2. Pour in the wine and top with the seltzer. Enjoy in peace.

Ronald Reagan

★ ★ ★ ★ ★

AMERICA IS
TOO GREAT
FOR SMALL
DREAMS.

★ ★ ★ ★ ★

RONALD REAGAN

REPUBLICAN | 1981–1989

❧ JELLY BEAN COSMO ❧

When Reagan became a politician, Jelly Belly began sending him shipments of free jelly beans. For his presidential inauguration, the brand shipped seven thousand pounds of red (very cherry), white (coconut), and blue (blueberry) jelly beans to Washington, DC. This cosmopolitanesque cocktail uses homemade jelly bean–infused vodka—a delicious allocation of resources by jelly bean–onomic standards.

Makes 1 drink

FOR THE JELLY BEAN VODKA:

¼ cup pomegranate, raspberry, or cherry jelly beans

½ cup vodka

FOR THE JELLY BEAN COSMO:

1 ounce Jelly Bean Vodka (see recipe)

1 ounce cranberry or pomegranate juice

¾ ounce Cointreau or triple sec

½ ounce fresh lime juice

1 lime wedge, for garnish

INSTRUCTIONS

1. **To make the Vodka:** Place the jelly beans in a resealable container and pour in the vodka. Cover and allow the vodka to sit at room temperature for 8 to 12 hours.

2. Strain the vodka through a fine-mesh sieve into a new container, discarding any sediment. Seal and refrigerate.

3. **To make the Cosmo:** Fill a cocktail shaker with ice and add the vodka, cranberry juice, Cointreau, and lime juice. Shake vigorously until chilled.

4. Strain into a chilled martini glass.

5. Garnish with a lime wedge and enjoy.

GEORGE H. W. BUSH

REPUBLICAN | 1989–1993

∽ BUSHWACKER ∾

The bushwacker was first concocted in 1975 in the U.S. Virgin Islands. A year later, George H. W. Bush became the director of central intelligence, a job that—like being president—probably makes a person want a drink at the end of the day. Sweet and creamy, this version of the cocktail blends rum, coffee, chocolate, and coconut flavors in an indulgent frozen drink that goes down easily.

★★★★★★★★★★★★★★★★★★ Makes 2 drinks ★★★★★★★★★★★★★★★★★★

INGREDIENTS

4 ounces lite coconut milk (from a can) or whole milk
2 ounces dark or spiced rum
2 ounces Kahlúa
2 ounces crème de cacao
1 ounce cream of coconut
1½ to 2 cups ice cubes
Ground nutmeg, for garnish

INSTRUCTIONS

1. Place the coconut milk, rum, Kahlúa, crème de cacao, cream of coconut, and ice in a blender and blend until smooth.

2. Divide the drink between two chilled glasses.

3. Garnish with a sprinkle of ground nutmeg and enjoy through straws.

* ★ ★ ★ *

BEING PRESIDENT IS LIKE RUNNING A CEMETERY: YOU'VE GOT A LOT OF PEOPLE UNDER YOU AND NOBODY'S LISTENING.

* ★ ★ ★ *

BILL CLINTON

DEMOCRAT | 1993–2001

∽ SOUTHERN SNAKEBITE ∽

Hailing from Hope, Arkansas, Bill Clinton became known for his charm and his languid, folksy way of public speaking, inspiring impressionists everywhere to master his unique Southern lilt. He was also known to love a traditional Snakebite (without the cordial). A rumor once surfaced that Clinton was refused the cocktail when he ordered one at a tavern in England, where the pub manager supposedly said, "It's illegal to serve them in the UK." However entertaining, both claims—that the manager said this and that it's illegal to serve them in the UK—were discovered to be false.

★ ★ ★ ★ ★ ★ ★ ★ ★ ★ ★ ★ ★ ★ ★ ★ ★ ★ Makes 1 drink ★ ★ ★ ★ ★ ★ ★ ★ ★ ★ ★ ★ ★ ★ ★ ★ ★ ★

INGREDIENTS

1 ounce blackcurrant cordial

6 ounces hard cider

6 ounces lager beer

INSTRUCTIONS

1. Pour the cordial into a chilled pint glass.

2. Add the hard cider and the lager.

3. Raise your glass and enjoy.

⋆ ⋆ ⋆ NO. 43 ⋆ ⋆ ⋆

GEORGE W. BUSH

REPUBLICAN | 2001–2009

∽ TEXAS RANCH WATER ∾

Having served as the governor of Texas from 1995 to 2000, Dubya—famously a sober president—brought to the White House an air of "you can take the politician out of Texas, but you can't take the Texas out of the politician." He and the former First Lady still own the 1,583-acre ranch outside of Crawford, Texas, where they challenge guests to join the 100-Degree Club, for which to qualify one must successfully run three miles in triple-digit heat. Ranch water, anyone?

⋆ ⋆ ⋆ ⋆ ⋆ ⋆ ⋆ ⋆ ⋆ ⋆ ⋆ ⋆ ⋆ ⋆ ⋆ **Makes 1 drink** ⋆ ⋆ ⋆ ⋆ ⋆ ⋆ ⋆ ⋆ ⋆ ⋆ ⋆ ⋆ ⋆ ⋆ ⋆

INGREDIENTS

2 1/2 ounces blanco tequila
3/4 ounce fresh lime juice
6 ounces sparkling mineral water
1 lime wedge, for garnish

INSTRUCTIONS

1. Fill a highball glass with ice and pour in the tequila and lime juice.

2. Top with the sparkling mineral water.

3. Garnish with the lime wedge and enjoy.

For an alcohol-free version, add a little more sparkling mineral water and lime, and leave out the tequila.

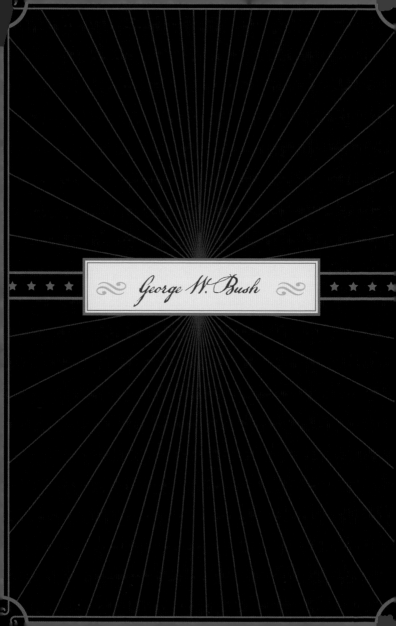

George W. Bush

★ ★ ★ ★ ★

SOME FOLKS

LOOK AT ME

AND SEE A

CERTAIN

SWAGGER,

WHICH IN TEXAS

IS CALLED

WALKING.

★ ★ ★ ★ ★

BARACK OBAMA

DEMOCRAT | 2009–2017

∿ BLUE HAWAIIAN ∿

Barack Obama stands as the first and only president to have hailed from Hawaii, the state where this vibrant, tropical cocktail was first created in 1957, just four years before the former Democratic president was born. A sweet and tart blend of pineapple and rum, shaken with creamy coconut, makes for a drink as cool as Obama himself.

★★★★★★★★★★★★★★★★★★★ Makes 1 drink ★★★★★★★★★★★★★★★★★★★

INGREDIENTS

3 ounces pineapple juice

1 1/2 ounces light rum

1 ounce cream of coconut

3/4 ounce blue curaçao

1 pineapple wedge, for garnish

1 maraschino cherry, for garnish

INSTRUCTIONS

1. Fill a cocktail shaker with ice and add the pineapple juice, rum, cream of coconut, and blue curaçao. Shake vigorously for five to seven chants of "yes we can," or until chilled.

2. Strain into a hurricane glass over crushed ice.

3. Garnish with the pineapple wedge and maraschino cherry, and enjoy through a straw.

DONALD J. TRUMP

REPUBLICAN | 2017–2021

⌘ SCREWDRIVER SBAGLIATO ⌘

You may be familiar with the negroni sbagliato, a cocktail that replaces the gin in a classic negroni with sparkling wine to make it "wrong," as the Italian word *sbagliato* directly translates to in English. But by mixing up this sparkly, extra-orangey take on a standard screwdriver, you can only go right.

★ ★ ★ ★ ★ ★ ★ ★ ★ ★ ★ ★ ★ ★ ★ Makes 1 drink ★ ★ ★ ★ ★ ★ ★ ★ ★ ★ ★ ★ ★ ★ ★

INGREDIENTS

1 1/2 ounces orange-flavored vodka

1/2 ounce triple sec

4 ounces sparkling orange soda (like Orangina or Sanpellegrino Aranciata)

1 orange slice, for garnish

INSTRUCTIONS

1. Fill a highball glass with ice and add the vodka and triple sec.

2. Top with the sparkling orange soda and stir to combine.

3. Garnish with the orange slice and enjoy while reading a classified document.

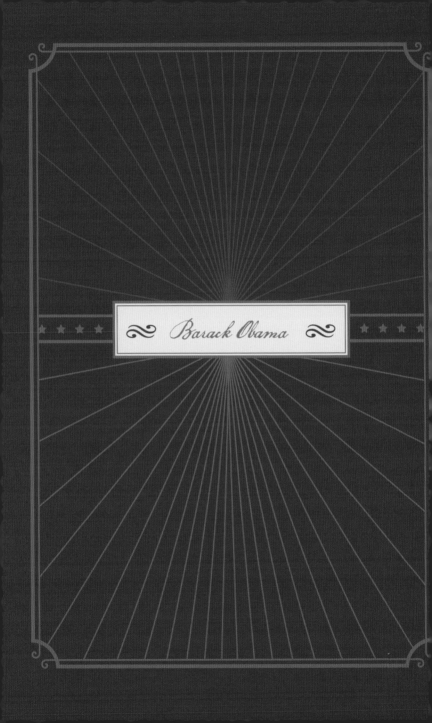

Barack Obama

* * ★ * *

BUT, THEN
AGAIN, THERE'S
NEVER A
BAD DAY
FOR A
BEER AND A
WEISSWURST.

* * ★ * *

JOE BIDEN

DEMOCRAT | 2021–

∽ JOEJITO ∽

Joe Biden has abstained from drinking his entire life, reportedly having never consumed an alcoholic beverage even once. As the oldest president to ever be elected, Biden doesn't shy away from balancing his political duties with good humor, exemplifying the fact that you don't need alcohol to have fun. This take on a classic Cuban mojito can easily be prepared as a mocktail.

★ ★ ★ ★ ★ ★ ★ ★ ★ ★ ★ ★ ★ ★ ★ Makes 1 drink ★ ★ ★ ★ ★ ★ ★ ★ ★ ★ ★ ★ ★ ★ ★

INGREDIENTS

4 fresh mint leaves

1 1/2 teaspoons unrefined cane sugar

3/4 ounce fresh lime juice

2 ounces silver rum

4 ounces lime-flavored sparkling mineral water

1 lime slice, for garnish

1 sprig fresh mint, for garnish

For a mocktail version of this classic, simply leave out the rum.

INSTRUCTIONS

1. Place the mint leaves, sugar, and lime juice in a highball glass. Muddle against the bottom of the glass for 25 to 30 seconds to release the mint's oils.

2. Fill the glass with crushed ice and pour in the rum.

3. Top with the sparkling mineral water and stir to combine.

4. Garnish with the lime slice and sprig of mint, and enjoy.

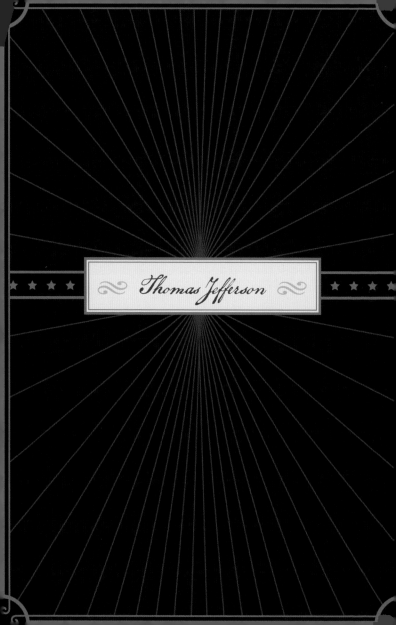

Thomas Jefferson

★ ★ ★ ★ ★

I THINK IT IS A

GREAT ERROR

TO CONSIDER A HEAVY

TAX ON WINES.

★ ★ ★ ★ ★

DEMOCRATIC

⌠ DONKEY PUNCH ⌡

The donkey was first associated with the Democratic Party during Andrew Jackson's 1828 campaign, when he printed a donkey on posters as a rebuttal to his non-supporters calling him a jackass. It wasn't until the 1870s that the donkey and elephant became popularized political symbols, thanks to the work of cartoonist Thomas Nast. It's not known when Donkey Punch became popular in American tiki bars, but it's soon to be a favorite in your home.

Makes 1 drink

INGREDIENTS

2 ounces orange juice

1 ounce pineapple juice

1 ounce rum or vodka

1/4 ounce grenadine

2 ounces ginger ale

1 maraschino or cocktail
   cherry, for garnish

INSTRUCTIONS

1. Fill a cocktail shaker with ice and add the orange juice, pineapple juice, rum, and grenadine. Shake vigorously until chilled.

2. Strain into a highball glass over fresh ice. Add the ginger ale and stir to combine.

3. Garnish with the cherry and enjoy through a straw.

To make an 8-serving batch, stir together 2 cups orange juice, 1 cup pineapple juice, 1 cup rum, and 1/4 cup grenadine in a pitcher or punch bowl filled with ice. Add 2 cups ginger ale right before serving.

And to make this a mocktail, simply leave out the rum.

DEMOCRATIC

~ FROZEN BLUE LAGOON ~

Whether you lean blue or red, we can all appreciate a cold, boozy slushy. Lemonade, vodka, and blue curaçao blend into a puckery-sweet drink that's vibrantly colored and generously sized. If you prefer your cocktails on the rocks, this is also delicious shaken and served over crushed ice, as shown here.

Makes 2 drinks

INGREDIENTS

12 ounces lemonade

3 ounces vodka

3 ounces blue curaçao

1½ to 2 cups ice cubes

6 fresh blueberries, for garnish

2 lemon slices, for garnish

INSTRUCTIONS

1. Place the lemonade, vodka, blue curaçao, and ice cubes in a blender and blend until smooth. Divide between two hurricane glasses.

2. Skewer three blueberries onto each of two toothpicks and rest them on the glasses, along with the lemon slice on each. Enjoy through straws.

For a single Blue Lagoon on the rocks, shown here, shake 6 ounces lemonade, 1½ ounces vodka, and 1½ ounces blue curaçao together in an ice-filled shaker until chilled. Strain into a hurricane glass over crushed ice.

REPUBLICAN

∾ THE RED TIDE ∾

A bit sweet, a bit tart, with hints of licorice, this burgundy-hued combination of flavors is an unexpected win.

★★★★★★★★★★★★★★★★ Makes 1 drink ★★★★★★★★★★★★★★★★

INGREDIENTS
2 ounces cranberry juice
1 ounce Jägermeister
1 ounce peach schnapps

INSTRUCTIONS
1. Fill a cocktail shaker with ice and add the cranberry juice, Jägermeister, and peach schnapps. Shake vigorously until chilled.
2. Strain into a rocks glass over fresh ice and enjoy.

REPUBLICAN

GRAND OLD PARTINI

Regardless of your political affiliation, we can all admit that a "grand old party" sounds like fun. Certainly more fun than a regular old party. With one of these double-alcohol, subtly orange martinis in hand, you can consider yourself a top candidate for having a good time.

Makes 1 drink

INGREDIENTS

1 ounce vodka

1 ounce gin

1 ounce Grand Marnier

½ ounce dry vermouth

1 orange twist, for garnish

INSTRUCTIONS

1. Fill a cocktail shaker with ice and add the vodka, gin, Grand Marnier, and vermouth. Shake vigorously until chilled.

2. Strain into a chilled martini glass.

3. Garnish with the orange twist and enjoy.

INDEPENDENT

UNCLE SAM'S APPLE PIEBALL

Republican, Democrat, or Independent, we can all agree on one thing: there are few things more American than apple pie. Lightly sweet and warmly spiced, this drink harnesses all the flavors of the classic dessert. You may even want to double the recipe and use a bigger glass—it'd be the American thing to do.

Makes 1 drink

INGREDIENTS

1 tablespoon granulated sugar

3/4 teaspoon ground cinnamon

Dash of salt

1 ounce vanilla vodka

3/4 ounce cinnamon whiskey

4 ounces apple cider

Apple slices, for garnish

INSTRUCTIONS

1. Mix the sugar, cinnamon, and salt together and pour onto a small plate.
2. Add a bit of water to a separate plate.
3. Dip the rim of a highball glass in the water, then in the cinnamon sugar, rotating the glass to create a thickly coated rim. Carefully fill with fresh ice and set aside.
4. Pour the vanilla vodka, cinnamon whiskey, and apple cider into a cocktail shaker filled with ice. Shake vigorously until chilled.
5. Strain into the rimmed glass.
6. Garnish with the apple slices and enjoy.

BIBLIOGRAPHY

"10 Birthday Facts About President Herbert Hoover."
National Constitution Center. August 10, 2023. https://
constitutioncenter.org.

"10 Fascinating Facts on President Ronald Reagan's Birthday."
National Constitution Center. February 6, 2023. https://
constitutioncenter.org.

Adams, John. "From John Adams to Caroline Amelia Smith De
Windt, 24 January 1820." National Archives. https://www
.archives.gov.

Baker, Jean H. "Franklin Pierce: Foreign Affairs." University of
Virginia: Miller Center. https://millercenter.org.

Brown, Larry. "Remembering and Appreciating Our Most
Intelligent President." *Cape Cod Times*. July 27, 2018. https://
www.capecodtimes.com.

Campbell, Jack. "John Adams's Love of Cider." *Journal of
the American Revolution*. November 24, 2021. https://
allthingsliberty.com.

"Chester A. Arthur." History.com. Updated June 10, 2019.
https://www.history.com.

"Chester Alan Arthur: Obscure or Underrated?" National
Constitution Center. October 5, 2022. https://
constitutioncenter.org.

"The Clinton Presidency: A Historic Era of Progress and
Prosperity." https://clintonwhitehouse5.archives.gov/index
.html.

Elder, Kara. "Recipes for Presidents' Day, from William H. Taft's Breakfast Cocktail to Melania Trump's Sugar Cookies." *The Washington Post*. February 16, 2017. https://www .washingtonpost.com.

"First Families." White House. https://www.whitehouse.gov.

"'I Think the American Public Wants a Solemn Ass as a President—and I Think I'll go Along with Them'—Calvin Coolidge." The Library of Congress. https://www.loc.gov.

"James A Garfield." *The Independent*. January 18, 2009. https:// www.independent.co.uk/us.

"James K. Polk - Administration." World Biography U.S. Presidents. https://www.presidentprofiles.com.

Klein, Christopher. "A Brief History of Presidential Drinking." History.com. Updated November 1, 2023. https://www .history.com.

"Knowing the Presidents: John Tyler." Smithsonian. https://www .si.edu.

"List of nicknames of presidents of the United States." Wikipedia. Accessed October 17, 2023. https://en.wikipedia.org/wiki /Main_Page.

Olver, Lynne. "American Presidents' Food Favorites." The Food Timeline. Updated February 4, 2022. www.foodtimeline.org /presidents.html.

"President Ford's Leadership." Gerald R. Ford Presidential Library & Museum. https://www.fordlibrarymuseum.gov /index.aspx.

"Presidential Favorite Desserts." *Wilton* (blog). Wilton. February 19, 2018. blog.wilton.com/presidential-favorite-desserts.

"Presidential Historians Survey 2021." C-SPAN. https://www .c-span.org.

"Presidents." White House. https://www.whitehouse.gov.

Ratcliffe, Susan, ed. *Oxford Essential Quotations* (5th edition). Oxford University Press. OxfordReference.com. Published online 2017. https://www.oxfordreference.com.

"The Senate Overrides the President's Veto of the Volstead Act." United States Senate. Accessed September 8, 2023. https://www.senate.gov/index.htm.

Smith, Gary Scott. "William McKinley: America as God's Instrument." In *Religion in the Oval Office: The Religious Lives of American Presidents*, 159–95. Oxford University Press eBooks, 2015. https://academic.oup.com.

Spetter, Allan B. "Benjamin Harrison: Campaigns and Elections." University of Virginia: Miller Center. https://millercenter.org.

"Thomas Jefferson Papers, 1606 to 1827." Library of Congress. https://www.loc.gov.

"Voices, Votes, Victory: Presidential Campaign Songs." Library of Congress. https://www.loc.gov.

Washington, George. "From George Washington to the Protestant Episcopal Church, Wednesday, August 19, 1789." Mountvernon.org. Accessed January 17, 2024. https://www.mountvernon.org.

Wells, Shari. "Remembering President Chester A. Arthur and First Lady Ellen Lewis Herndon Arthur." *Please Be Seated!* (blog). August 4, 2011. https://pleasebeseated.wordpress.com.

"Which president was known as 'The Little Magician?'" David Bruce Smith's Grateful American Foundation. https://gratefulamericanfoundation.org.

"Which President, Which Drink." Vivino. October 20, 2020. https://www.vivino.com.

Will-Weber, Mark. "A complete list of every president's favorite drink." *New York Post*. Updated January 1, 2018. https://nypost.com.

'TIS WELL.

★ ★ ★ ★ ★ *George Washington*